Grandmother and Friends Olde Time Easy Cooking

Dear Echo & Steve —
— This cook book was compiled
by your 3th cousin — Your dad's
brother daughter — You ~~met~~ met
her in St Louis — 48th years ago.

Ms Joyce K Holcomb

With love

Mom

12-12-12

ISBN: 1477630120
ISBN 13: 9781477630129

Acknowledgements

My two wonderful grandmothers, Norma Lemmon Holcomb and Ann Pansic Relic, both loved to cook and enjoyed sharing recipes with family and friends. I have recorded their recipes in this book. Some additional recipes included in this book have come from various family members and friends which I have obtained over the years. Credit cannot be given to all the contributors due to the fact names were not attached to old hand written recipe cards or pieces of paper.

I was fortunate to have two sets of grandparents growing up. But my grandmothers were women before their time. Grandmother Holcomb raised 3 children, a daughter, Dorothy Lamm and two sons, Jack and James Leroy (Lee) during the depression and had to rely on foods from the garden, she and granddad planted. During World War II, she worked on the production line at Standard Oil Company in Wood River, Illinois along with her sister-in-law, Hattie Holcomb and without knowing it her future daughter-in-law, Dorothy. As a child, I remember picking green beans from the garden and sitting with my grandmother and snapping the beans apart. Grandmother would always have food cooking in the kitchen. I can remember the aroma of cakes, pies, cookies and good food being prepared. She always had a box of Bisquick handy. This is a lost art today.

Grandmother Relic raised two daughters, my mother Dorothy Holcomb and Joan Relic Denney in a small coal mining town of Masontown, Pennsylvania during the depression before moving to Wood River, Illinois and owning a restaurant called, Ann's Café in Wood River. She was used to cooking for multiple people at one time or for the extended family. Later in life, grandmother worked on a "dude ranch" in Rim Rock, Arizona just north of Wickenburg, Arizona. She ensured there was always food on the table for the ranchers and guests. I remember that when grandmother cooked, it was always in large pots and pans because she never knew who might stop by for a visit and she always wanted to have food available to offer her family and friends. Grandmother always had a garden and fruit trees in the backyard, where she would gather the fruits and vegetables to prepare the meals. She would also give items from her garden to family, friends, and neighbors.

I know the ingredients used in some of these recipes will make people sit up and think, fixing most things from scratch and using ingredients, like, shortening or by other names, lard along with butter, baking soda and other ingredients which are not considered "healthy" today. But I have to tell you, both of my grandmothers and grandfathers lived very long healthy lives, Grandmother Holcomb was 81 and Grandmother Relic was 96. I believe these recipes were enjoyed by not only them, but also by their families and friends and of course, me. I hope you enjoy them too!

Joyce Holcomb

DEDICATED TO:

My grandmothers, Norma and Ann

Table of Contents

Beverages

Here are several simple and easy beverages to use at parties, showers, weddings, on picnics' or family gatherings.

Wedding Ring Punch

- 2 Pints lemon sherbet
- 2 Tablespoons maraschino cherry juice
- 3 Cups chilled ginger ale
- ¼ Cup lemon juice
- ½ Cup pineapple juice
- 1 6 ounce can frozen orange juice, diluted

Steps:

1. Pack sherbet into a 1 quart ring mold and freeze
2. Combine lemon, pineapple, orange and maraschino cherry juice and mix well
3. Chill mixture

To Serve:

1. Pour juice mixture into punch bowl and add ginger ale
2. Unmold sherbet ring by turning mold upside down on a plate and pressing hot cloths around it
3. Slip sherbet ring into punch bowl and garnish with fresh strawberries or mint springs

Yields: 16 punch cups

Fruited Ice Cubes

- 1 No. 2 ½ can fruit cocktail
- 2 Tablespoons lemon juice
- 1 Cup water

Steps:

1. Mix ingredients
2. Pour into ice cube trays and freeze

Summer Fruit Punch

- 2 Cups strong hot tea
- 1 ½ Cups orange juice
- ½ Cup sugar
- ½ Cup lemon juice
- 4 Cups apricot nectar
- 1 Quart ginger ale

Steps:

1. Make tea
2. Then add sugar, lemon juice, orange juice and apricot nectar
3. Chill thoroughly and add ginger ale
4. Pour over fruited ice cubes in tall chilled glasses

Orange Crush (serve with or without alcohol)

- 1 6 ounce can frozen concentrated orange juice
- ½ Pint orange sherbet ice cream
- 1 7 ounce bottle ginger ale, chilled
- 1 Cup ice cubes

Steps:

1. Reconstitute orange juice according to label directions
2. Put into electric blender or shaker
3. Add remaining ingredients
4. Blend or shake until thick and frothy

To Serve:

1. Pour into six tall chilled glasses garnish with mint
2. Optional: Add: 1 cup of rum, whiskey or vodka for an alcoholic drink

Pool Side Cooler (serve with or without alcohol)

- 1 6 ounce can frozen concentrated orange juice
- 1 6 ounce can frozen strawberries
- 1 6 ounce can frozen lemon
- 1 Pint fresh strawberries
- 2 Cups ice cubes

Steps:

1. Combine and blend all ingredients except fresh strawberries
2. Serve in chilled wine glasses

To Serve:

1. Garnish with sliced fresh strawberries or mint
2. Optional: Add: 1 cup of rum, whiskey or vodka for an alcoholic drink

Cakes and Frostings

To cut a fresh cake, heat a thin knife in boiling water, dry it, and you can cut the thinnest of pieces.

Apple Sauce Cake

- 2 Cups <u>Hot</u> applesauce
- ½ Cup shortening
- 3 Teaspoons baking soda
- 2 Cups sifted flour
- 2 Cups sugar
- 1 Cup raisins or dates
- 1 Teaspoon nutmeg
- 1 Teaspoon cloves
- 1 Teaspoon cinnamon
- Pinch of salt

Steps:

1. Mix all the above ingredients together and be sure the apple sauce is <u>hot</u>.
2. Bake in 9 x 13 inch baking dish (greased and floured)
3. Bake at 350^0F for 30 to 35 minutes

To Serve:

1. Set and let cool
2. Serve with whipped cream or ice cream

Red Chocolate Cake

- ½ Cup Cocoa
- 2 Teaspoons baking soda
- ½ Cup water
- 1 Cup buttermilk
- 2 Teaspoons vanilla

- ¾ Cup shortening
- 1 ½ Cups sugar
- 2 Whole Eggs
- 2 ½ cups flour

Steps:

1. Combine, cocoa, baking soda and water; let set while mixing other ingredients
2. Cream shortening, sugar and eggs together
3. Then add buttermilk, vanilla and flour
4. Then combine all ingredients together
5. Pour into 3-8 inches greased and floured round layer pans
6. Bake at 375°F for 30 minutes
7. Let set and cool
8. Use your favorite frosting

To Serve:

1. Serve with ice cream or fresh fruit

Fruit Cocktail Crisp

- 1 Number 2 ½ can fruit cocktail, drain well
- 1 Cup flour
- 1 Cup sugar
- 1 Teaspoon salt
- 1 Teaspoon baking soda
- ½ Cup brown sugar
- ½ Cup chopped nuts (optional)

Steps:

1. Mix dry ingredients and combine with drained fruit, except brown sugar and nuts
2. Put into 8 x 8 inch or 6 x 10 inch greased and floured baking dish
3. Sprinkle ½ cup brown sugar over top of batter
4. Optional topping: add – ½ cup chopped nuts
5. Bake at 350°F for 60 minutes

To Serve:

1. Serve plain or with whipped cream

Blackberry Jam Cake

- 1 Cup butter
- 2 Cups sugar
- 1 Cup buttermilk
- 1 Teaspoon baking soda
- 4 Egg yolks, beaten
- 3 Cups sifted flour
- 1 Teaspoon vanilla

- 1 Teaspoon nutmeg
- 1 Teaspoon cloves
- 1 Teaspoon allspice
- 1 Cup blackberry jam or preserves
- 4 Eggs whites, beaten
- 2 Teaspoons cinnamon

Steps:

1. Cream butter and gradually add sugar
2. Dissolve baking soda in buttermilk and add eggs yolks
3. Alternate this mixture with dry ingredients to creamed butter and sugar
4. Add vanilla, jam or preserves
5. Fold in egg whites
6. Bake in 3-8 inch greased and floured round layer pans at 350^0F for 30 minutes

To Serve:

1. Layers will be moist
2. Let set and cool
3. Ice with whipped cream between layers or your favorite frosting

Apple Torte

- 1 ¾ Cups flour
- ½ Pound butter
- 2 Teaspoons baking powder
- 1 Can apples or 8 large apples
- 2 Cups sugar
- 4 Eggs

Steps:

1. Add 1 cup of sugar to ¼ pound melted butter and beat well
2. Add 2 eggs, mix thoroughly
3. Add dry ingredients and beat well
4. Spread on bottom of a greased and floured spring form pan
5. Pare apples and cut in eights and stand them on end
6. Sprinkle with cinnamon and bake at 350°F for 60 minutes
7. In separate bowl, cream ¼ pound butter and 1 cup sugar and add 2 eggs
8. Mix thoroughly
9. Pour over top of baked torte and bake at 325°F for additional 15 minutes

Cheese Cake Tarts

- 1 6 ounces Philadelphia cream cheese, softened
- 1 Teaspoon lemon juice
- ¾ Cup sugar
- 2 Eggs
- 1 Teaspoon vanilla
- 12 vanilla wafers

Steps:

1. Mix all ingredients together
2. Pour into paper lined muffin tin with a vanilla wafer place in the bottom
3. Bake at 375°F for 15 minutes

To Serve:

1. Let set and cool
2. Top each cheese cake with a spoonful of your favorite pie filling, cherry, peach or blueberry

Fruit Cocktail Cake

- 2 Cups flour
- 2 Cups sugar
- 2 Pinches cinnamon
- 2 Teaspoons baking soda

- 2 Teaspoons salt
- 1 Large can fruit cocktail and juice
- 2 Eggs, well beaten

Steps:

1. Mix, flour, sugar, cinnamon, baking soda, salt together
2. Add and stir well, fruit cocktail with juice
3. Add eggs well beaten
4. Pour into 10x14 inch greased and floured baking dish
5. Sprinkle topping of 1 cup of brown sugar and 1 cup of chopped nuts (optional) before baking
6. Bake at 300^{0}F for 80 minutes

To Serve:

1. Let set and cool
2. Serve with whipped cream or ice cream

Triple Chocolate Cake

- 1 Box chocolate cake mix
- 1 Large Package chocolate pudding – NOT INSTANT PUDDING
- 2 Cups chocolate chips – small
- 1 Cup chopped walnuts (optional)

Steps:

1. Cook pudding as directed on box
2. Prepare cake mix with chocolate chips and add to warm pudding and mix well
3. Pour into greased and floured 13 x 9 inch baking dish or 2-8 inch round layer pans
4. Bake at 350^0F for 40 minutes

To Serve:

1. Serve warm topped with whipped cream or cooled sprinkled with powdered sugar
2. Can be frosted but it is very, very rich

Caramel Icing

- 1 Cup brown sugar, firmly packed
- 3 Tablespoons butter
- 1 Tablespoon shortening
- ¼ Cup milk
- 1 Cup powdered sugar

Steps:

1. Place brown sugar, butter and shortening in sauce pan
2. Melt over low heat and stir constantly
3. Add milk
4. Boil for 3 minutes
5. Cool slightly and then add powdered sugar
6. Beat until thick

Whipped Cream Frosting

- 2 Tablespoons flour
- ½ Cup milk
- ¼ Cup butter
- ¼ Cup shortening
- ½ Cup sugar
- 1 Teaspoon vanilla or almond

Steps:

1. Mix flour and milk in sauce pan
2. Cook over low heat until thick
3. Put in bowl and cool
4. In separate bowl, cream butter and shortening for 4 minutes with electric beater
5. Add sugar gradually and beat for 4 minutes
6. After flour paste is cold add to mixture and beat 4 more minutes
7. Add vanilla and blend

Ann's Marshmallow Frosting

- ¼ Teaspoon salt
- 2 Eggs whites
- ¼ Cup sugar
- ¾ Cup Karo syrup (red or blue label)
- 1 ¼ Teaspoons vanilla

Steps:

1. Add salt to egg whites and beat until frothy
2. Gradually add sugar beating until smooth and glossy
3. Slowly add Karo syrup and continue beating until frosting stands in firm peaks
4. Fold in vanilla

Flavor Variations: Add 2 tablespoons cocoa or 1 Tablespoon grated orange or lemon rind with Karo syrup in place of vanilla

Norma's Frosting

- 4 Tablespoons butter
- 2 ½ Cups confectioner's sugar, sift before measuring
- 2 Eggs whites
- ½ Teaspoon vanilla

Steps:

1. Cream butter
2. Add 1 cup of the sugar slowly, beating constantly
3. In separate bowl, beat the egg whites stiff
4. Add the remaining 1 ½ cup sugar, beating it in gradually
5. Combine the two mixtures until the consistency of whipped cream
6. Add the vanilla

Never Fail Icing

- 1 Cup sugar
- 3 Tablespoons water
- 2 Eggs whites
- ½ Teaspoon cream tartar
- 1 Teaspoon vanilla
- Pinch of salt

Steps:

1. Place all ingredients in the top of a double boiler pan
2. Place over hot water and beat until icing will stand in stiff peaks

Casseroles

Before cooking rice, grease the pan with butter or put
a piece of butter in the rice and it will not stick to
the pan as it so often does.

Stuffed Peppers

- 6 to 8 Hot wax red or green peppers, medium size
- 1 Pound pork
- 1 Pound veal
- ½ Cup rice
- 1 Egg
- ¼ Teaspoon black pepper
- 1 Small onion chopped, fine
- 1 ½ Teaspoons salt
- 1 Can large tomatoes
- ½ Can water
- 1 Tablespoon shortening
- 2 Tablespoons flour

Steps:

1. Wash and remove the stem and seeds from peppers
2. Mix all ingredients together except tomatoes, shortening and flour and pour small amount of water to make mixture not too thick
3. When these ingredients are mixed thoroughly stuff each pepper with meat
4. All excess meat can be made into small balls and placed in casserole with peppers
5. Use a small roaster or casserole for cooking
6. Place the peppers and meat balls in casserole
7. Pour large can tomatoes plus ½ can water over all
8. Bake at 350^{0}F for 2 to 2 ½ hours
9. Just before done make a thickening of about 1 tablespoon shortening and 2 Tablespoon flour
10. Mix this in small pan and brown slightly
11. Pour over casserole and return to oven for 10 to 15 minutes

To Serve:

1. Serve plain or with sour cream

Yankee Doodle Macaroni

- 1 Cup minced onion
- 1 Clove garlic
- 3 Tablespoons butter
- 1 Pound ground beef
- ¾ Cup mushrooms
- 3 ½ Cups tomatoes

Steps:

1. Cook minced onion and clove garlic in 3 tablespoons butter until yellow
2. Add ground beef, mushrooms and cook until brown
3. Then add tomatoes, parsley salt and pepper to taste
4. Bake 350^{0}F for 60 minutes

To Serve:

Serve over hot boiled long macaroni

Stuffed Ham Roll

- ½ Pound of slice ham, ¼ Inch thick slices
- 1 Egg, slightly beaten
- 1 Cup dry bread crumbs
- Milk to moisten
- 1 ½ teaspoons salt
- 1 ¼ Cups lima beans, soaked and boiled
- ¼ Teaspoon mustard
- 1 Tablespoon brown sugar
- Dash of pepper

Steps:

1. Make dressing of bread crumbs, ¼ teaspoon salt, dash of pepper, mustard, egg and milk
2. Spread dressing on ham slices and tie with cooking cord or string
3. Place in baking dish and surround with beans
4. Add 1 ½ teaspoons salt and brown sugar
5. Cover and bake at 350^0F until done adding water if necessary
6. Remove lid during latter part of cooking to brown

John's Oven Baked Picnic Chicken

- 1 Large whole chicken
- 1 Cup shortening
- ½ Cup flour
- 4 Eggs
- 3 Cups milk
- Dash of salt

Steps:

1. Cook chicken until its falls from the bone
2. In separate bowl, mix all the ingredients together
3. Cook until slightly thick – makes dressing
4. Alternate layers of chicken and dressing in greased baking dish
5. Bake 375°F for 50 to 60 minutes

Green Bean Casserole

- 1 Can mushrooms
- 1 Can mushroom buttons
- 2 Packages frozen French style green beans
- 1 Small package sharp cheddar cheese
- 1 Small package bread crumbs

Steps:

1. Combine mushrooms and mushroom buttons
2. Cook slightly till warm
3. Add frozen French style green beans
4. Add sharp cheddar cheese for taste
5. Put bread crumbs on top
6. Bake at 350^0F for 20 minutes

Shrimp Therimodar

- 1 Can frozen shrimp soup * or cream of shrimp soup
- 2 Tablespoons butter
- 1 Package frozen shrimp
- ¼ Cup milk
- 1 4 ounce can mushrooms
- ¼ Teaspoon mustard
- ½ Pound sharp cheddar cheese, grated

Steps:

1. Thaw soup in bowl or prepared substitute cream of shrimp soup
2. Add milk and shrimp
3. Brown mushrooms in butter and add to shrimp
4. Mix all ingredients together adding in cheddar cheese
5. Add a dash of paprika and dash of red pepper and salt to taste
6. Bake at 400^0F for 15 minutes

To Serve:

Serve over cooked rice

*Frozen shrimp soup may not be available today at the supermarkets so substitute cream of shrimp soup

Deviled Macaroni Deluxe

- 1 8 ounce package macaroni, cooked and drained
- 1 10 ½ ounce can cream of mushroom soup
- ¼ Cup milk
- 1 Cup grated sharp cheese
- ¼ Cup pimento, diced
- 1 Teaspoon onion salt
- ¼ Teaspoon pepper
- 2 Teaspoons mustard
- 4 Hard boiled eggs, sliced
- ¼ Cup dry bread crumbs
- 2 Tablespoons melted butter

Steps:

1. Combine macaroni, soup, milk, cheese, pimento and seasonings
2. Spoon ½ mixture into a buttered casserole dish
3. Add layer of sliced eggs, top with remaining mixture
4. Mix bread crumbs with butter, sprinkle over casserole
5. Bake at 350°F for 40 minutes
6. Garnish with sliced eggs

Chicken Casserole with sauce

Ingredients for chicken casserole:

- 1 4 Pounds chicken (2 cups meat)
- 2 Cups fresh bread crumbs
- 1 Cup cooked rice (measured after cooking)
- 1 ½ Teaspoons salt
- ⅛ Cup chopped pimento
- 3 Cups milk, chicken broth or half and half
- 4 Well beaten eggs

Steps:

1. Mix all above ingredients together adding eggs last
2. Bake at 325^0F for 60 minutes

Ingredients for Sauce:

- ¼ Cup butter
- ¼ Cup mushrooms or 1 small can
- ¼ Cup flour
- 1 Pint chicken broth
- ¼ Cup cream, if desired
- Dash of paprika
- ½ Teaspoon chopped parsley
- ½ Teaspoon lemon juice
- Salt to taste

Steps:

1. Melt the butter in sauce pan and add flour and mix well
2. Add chicken broth and stir constantly till thick and smooth
3. Add other ingredients
4. Let stand over hot water till ready to serve

To Serve:

1. Spoon over chicken loaf

Hamburger Upside-Down Bake

- 1 Pound hamburger
- ¼ Cup chopped onion
- 1 Teaspoon salt
- ½ Teaspoon chili powder, optional
- 1 Bottle ketchup
- 1 Can 12 ounce golden whole kernel corn
- 1 Package corn muffin meal mix (8 ounce box)

Steps:

1. In a 10 inch skillet with oven-proof or removable handle, combine: first 4 ingredients, hamburger, chopped onion, salt, chili powder (optional) with ½ cup ketchup
2. Be sure to use 10 inch skillet or corn bread layer will be too thick
3. Break meat apart with fork: fry until just brown
4. Push meat back around edge of skillet
5. Spread undrained corn in center
6. In separate bowl, mix muffin batter as directed on package
7. Pour muffin batter evenly over corn and meat
8. Bake at 425°F about 15 to 20 minutes or until muffin layer is done

To Serve:

1. Let stand 5 minutes and turn out upside down on warm serving plate
2. Heat rest of ketchup and serve as a sauce

Eggplant Casserole

- 4 Cups eggplant – sliced thin
- 10 Ounces provolone cheese – sliced
- 8 Ounces mozzarella cheese – shredded
- 1 Pound lean ground beef
- ½ Cup chopped onion
- 3 Cloves garlic – sliced
- 1 Cup mushrooms – sliced
- ½ Cup celery – chopped
- 1 Teaspoon Italian seasoning
- 1 16 Ounce jar spaghetti sauce

Steps:

1. Saute lean ground beef in frying pan with mushrooms, garlic, onion, celery and Italian seasoning
2. Fry until the meat is no longer pink
3. Drain any excess oil and remove
4. Peel eggplant and slice it very thin
5. Grease and flour bottom and sides of a 9 x 13 inch baking dish
6. Layer half the eggplant on the bottom of the dish
7. Sprinkle eggplant with additional seasoning if desired
8. Layer half of the meat mixture, half of the sauce and half of the provolone cheese (lasagna style)
10. Repeat layering with the remaining ingredients
11. Spread mozzarella over the top of the casserole, cover with foil
12. Bake at 350°F for approximately 45 minutes or until done, remove the foil for the last 5 to 10 minutes to brown

Cookies

To prevent cookies, cakes and pies from burning on the bottom, sprinkle the bottom of the oven with fine dry salt.

Old Fashioned Soft Molasses Cookies

- 3 Cups flour
- ½ Teaspoon baking powder
- ¾ Teaspoon ginger
- ½ Teaspoon cinnamon
- ½ Teaspoon salt
- ½ Cup shortening
- 1 Cup brown sugar (packed)
- 2 Eggs
- ½ Teaspoon Baking soda
- ¾ Cup hot water
- ½ Cup dark molasses

Steps:

1. Sift flour, measure and resift baking powder, ginger, cinnamon and salt, 3 times and set aside
2. In separate bowl, cream shortening and brown sugar thoroughly
3. Then add eggs, one at a time and beat mixture thoroughly after each addition
4. Stir in molasses
5. Stir in the flour mixture that was set aside
6. Then combine baking soda and water and add to mixture
7. Mix thoroughly
8. Drop by heaping teaspoonfuls onto greased baking sheet
9. Sprinkle with granulated sugar
10. Bake at 375°F for 8 to 10 minutes

Yields: 4 dozen

Butterscotch Brownies

½ Cup butter, melted
2 Cups brown sugar
2 Eggs
1 Cup flour

2 Teaspoons baking powder
¾ Teaspoon salt
1 Teaspoon vanilla
½ Nuts (optional)

Steps:

1. Mix in order given ingredients.
2. Pour in greased and floured 13 x 9 inch baking dish
3. Bake at 350°F for 20 to 25 minutes

Aunt Dot's Christmas Tree Cookies

- 1 Cup butter
- ½ Cup sugar
- 1 Teaspoon almond extract
- 2 ¼ Cups flour
- 1 Egg
- Cinnamon, several dashes

Steps:

1. Cream soft butter
2. Add sugar and beat until fluffy
3. Beat in egg and almond extract (can substitute vanilla extract or lemon extract)
4. Blend in flour
5. Add several dashes of cinnamon as blending in flour
6. Bake at 350°F for 8 to 10 minutes or until bottom of cookies are golden

Yields: 4 dozen

Recommend:

1. Chilling dough before filling cookie press
2. Can chill for 30 minutes or overnight. This makes filling the press a little easier and you can use small amount of flour on inside of cookie press cylinder. Fill cookie press with dough and form into desired shapes.
3. This recipe is used for the Christmas trees and holiday wreaths
4. If icing individual Christmas tree cookies use several dashes of green food coloring and mix with white icing
5. After icing Christmas trees, sprinkle with various decorations

Additional tips:

1. For Christmas wreaths, before filling cookie press, divide dough into thirds
2. Mix into divided dough a few drops of red and green food coloring leaving one third plain
3. For a rainbow effect, combine the color dough together
4. Normally, only use food coloring for the Christmas wreaths
5. Top holiday wreath with maraschino cherries (cut in half)
6. Can use green dough for Christmas trees and sprinkle with decorations before baking if not icing
7. If you freeze cookies, you can place in microwave for 5 to 7 seconds or until soft before serving

Christmas Mounds With Peanuts

- 1 6 ounce package chocolate chips
- 1 6 ounce package butterscotch chips
- 1 5 ounce can of Chinese chow mein noodles
- 1 Cup salted peanuts (optional)

Steps:

1. Melt chips in double boiler
2. Break up Chinese noodles
3. Add noodles and nuts (optional) and stir
4. Drop on wax paper and chill

Aunt Dot's Rum Balls with Nuts

- 1 Can evaporated milk
- 1 Package semi-sweet chocolate
- 2 ½ Cups vanilla wafers (about 50 to 60 crushed wafers)
- ½ Cup confectioner's sugar
- ⅓ Cup rum
- 1 ¼ Cup nuts (optional)

Steps:

1. Cook milk and chocolate over medium heat
2. Remove and add remaining ingredients
3. Let stand for 30 minutes
4. Spoon out dough onto cookie sheet
5. Bake at 350°F for 45 minutes

Old Fashion Cream Cookies

- 1 Cup butter
- 1 Cup white sugar
- 1 Cup brown sugar
- 1 Teaspoon vanilla
- 2 Eggs
- 1 Cup sour cream
- 4 Cups flour
- 1 Teaspoon baking soda
- 1 Teaspoon baking powder
- ½ Teaspoon salt

Steps:

1. Cream butter with white and brown sugars
2. Add vanilla, eggs and sour cream
3. Sift dry ingredients into this mixture
4. Chill for 3 hours
5. Roll out and cut, and sprinkle sugar on top
6. Bake at 350^0F for 12 to 15 minutes

Desserts

For a delicious substitute for whipped cream, add a sliced banana to the white of an egg and beat it until it is stiff, the banana will completely dissolve.

Striped Delights

- 1 Box graham crackers
- 8 Ounces cream cheese
- 1 Tub cool whip
- 2 Large boxes of instant chocolate pudding
- 1 Small cup chopped pecans (optional)
- 3 Cups milk

Steps for first layer:

1. Make graham cracker crust as directed on box for 9 inch pie crust
2. Spread on bottom of 13 x 9 inch baking dish or use readymade pie crust and cut this recipe in half

Steps for second layer:

1. Mix cream cheese with 1 cup of cool whip
2. Spread over crust

Steps for third layer:

1. Mix instant chocolate pudding with cold milk
2. Spread over second layer, Pudding will be thick

Steps for Topping:

1. Spread remaining cool whip over pudding and top with chopped pecan (optional)

To Serve:

1. Chill for several hours before cutting into dessert

Four Layer Pistachio Delight Torte

- 1 Cup flour
- ½ Cup chopped pecans (optional)
- ¼ Pound butter or margarine
- 8 Ounces cream cheese
- 1 Cup confectioner's sugar
- 2 Packages instant pistachio pudding
- 2 ⅔ Cups milk
- 1 Tub cool whip

Steps for first layer:

1. Blend flour, margarine or butter with chopped pecans (optional)
2. Press into 13 x 9 inch baking dish
3. Bake at 375°F for 12 minutes
4. Let cool

Steps for second layer:

1. Blend cream cheese (room temperature) with sugar
2. Add 1 cup cool whip
3. Beat until fluffy
4. Spread over bottom lay

Steps for third layer:

1. Combine 2 packages instant pistachio with milk
2. Spread over second layer

Steps for fourth layer:

1. Spread remainder of cool whip over layers
2. Garnish with chopped pecans (optional)

To Serve:

1. Chill 3 hours or overnight before cutting into dessert

Pink Freeze

- 2 3 ounce packages cream cheese
- 2 Tablespoons mayonnaise or salad dressing
- 2 Tablespoons sugar
- 2 Cups whole cranberry sauce
- 1 9 ounce can crushed pineapple, drained
- ½ Cup chopped walnuts (optional)
- 1 Cup whipping cream, whipped

Steps:

1. Soften cheese; blend in mayonnaise or salad dressing and sugar
2. Add fruits and nuts (optional)
3. Fold in whipped cream
4. Pour into 8 ½ x 4 ½ x 2 ½ inch meatloaf pan
5. Freeze firm for 6 hours or overnight

To Serve:

1. Let stand at room temperature about 15 minutes
2. Turn out on lettuce leaf and slice

Orange Dessert

1 16 ounces cottage cheese
1 Box orange Jello
1 Small can mandarin oranges, drained
1 Small can crushed pineapple, drained
4 Ounces cool whip

Steps:

1. Use a 13 x 9 inch baking dish
2. Mix cottage cheese, orange and pineapple together
3. Place mixture on bottom of baking dish
4. In separate bowl, prepare Jello as directed on box
5. Let Jello chill until almost firm then spread Jello on top of mixture
6. Spread cool whip or whipping cream as topping
7. Chill a few hours before serving

Strawberry Pretzel Jello Salad

- 2 Cups crushed salted twisted pretzels
- 3 Tablespoons sugar
- ¾ Cup melted butter
- 8 Ounces cream cheese
- 1 Cup sugar
- 8 Ounces cool whip
- 6 Ounces strawberry Jello
- 2 ½ Cups **Hot** water
- 1 16-24 ounces of frozen sweetened strawberries, thawed and drained

Note: Can substitute 2 ½ cups hot water by using 1 cup strawberry juice from thawed strawberries and only 1 ½ cups of hot water in step 3

Steps for first layer:

1. Mix pretzels, sugar and melted butter
2. Press into 13 x 9 inch baking dish
3. Bake at 400°F for 8 to 10 minutes
4. Let set and cool before starting 2nd layer

Steps for second layer:

1. Beat cream cheese, sugar and cool whip
2. Spread over cooled pretzel crust
3. This layer needs to be chilled before starting 3th layer

Steps for third layer:

1. Mix strawberry Jello and very **Hot** water: in place of 2 ½ cups hot water can use 1 cup drained strawberry juice and only 1 ½ cups of hot water
2. Then add thawed strawberries
3. Then cool in refrigerator until slightly thicken
4. Then spreading over cheese layer
5. Then refrigerate for several hours or overnight before serving

John's Mississippi River Pudding

- 2 Eggs
- 1 ½ Cups sugar
- 4 Tablespoons flour
- 2 ½ Teaspoons baking powder
- ¼ Teaspoon salt
- 1 Cup chopped nuts (optional)
- 1 Cup chopped apples
- 2 Teaspoons vanilla

Steps:

1. Beat eggs and sugar until very smooth
2. Combine flour, baking powder and salt
3. Stir into egg mixture
4. Add apples, nuts (optional) and vanilla
5. Baked in greased baking dish at 350°F for 35 minutes

To Serve:

Serve with whipped cream or ice cream

Ann's Pineapple-Lemon Dessert

- 1 Package lemon Jello
- 1 ½ Cups water
- ½ Cup sugar
- 1 Tall can crushed pineapple, drained
- 1 Tall can Pet milk, whipped stiff
- 1 Box vanilla wafers, crushed
- 1 Lemon, juice and rind

Steps:

1. Mix above ingredients
2. Butter baking dish and line with half of crushed vanilla wafers
3. Put mixture in baking dish and place remaining crushed vanilla wafers on top
4. Chill for several hours

Meat Dishes

To save left over onions, slice then toast in the oven to a golden brown. Store in a tightly covered jar. Good for sprinkling over meats and stews.

Barbecued Spare Ribs

- 4 Pounds spare ribs
- 1 Cup ketchup
- ⅓ Cup Worcestershire Sauce
- 1 Teaspoon chili powder
- 1 Teaspoon salt
- 2 Cups water
- 2 Dashes Tabasco Sauce
- 3 Lemons
- 2 Large onions

Steps:

1. Wipe spare ribs with a clean, damp cloth
2. Cut into pieces 3 ribs wide
3. Place in large roasting pan, meat side up
4. Put lemon slices and onion slices on each section
5. Bake at 450^0F for 30 minutes
6. In separate saucepan, combine above ingredients and stir well to blend
7. Bring slowly to a boil
8. Pour over ribs and cover
9. Lower temperature to 350^0F, cover and bake 45 minutes basting with sauce every 10 to 15 minutes
10. Then uncover and bake 15 minutes longer

Salmon Loaf

- 1 Large can pink salmon
- 1 Teaspoon salt
- ½ Teaspoon pepper
- ½ Cup hot milk
- ¼ Teaspoon paprika
- 2 Tablespoons lemon juice
- 2 Egg yolks
- ½ Cup cracker crumbs
- 3 Eggs whites

Steps:

1. Mix salmon (mash it fine) add salt and all other ingredients
2. Fold in egg whites which have been beaten stiff
3. Pour into well buttered loaf pan
4. Bake at 350°F for 60 minutes

BAR-B-Q Chicken

- 5 -6 Pieces of chicken
- $\frac{1}{3}$ Cup celery
- 2 Tablespoons brown sugar
- $\frac{1}{2}$ Teaspoon lemon juice
- $\frac{1}{2}$ Teaspoon mustard or grey poupon
- 2 Cans tomato sauce
- $\frac{1}{2}$ Cup water

Steps:

1. Mix the above ingredients and sprinkle over chicken in a baking dish
2. Bake at 350°F for 75 minutes

Mother's Sunday Pork Chops

6	Lean pork chops
6	Tablespoons raw rice
1	Large onion
2	Tomatoes
1	Green pepper
3	Cups hot water

Steps:

1. Sear the chops on both sides
2. Arrange in a casserole dish or baking dish
3. Place on top of each chop: 1 tablespoon of rice, one slice of tomato, two strips green pepper, one slice onion
4. Cover with hot water, adding salt and pepper for seasoning
5. Bake at 350°F for 60 minutes or until done

Chicken Rice Hot Dinner

5-6 Pieces of chicken
1 Can crème of celery soup
1 Can crème of mushroom soup
1 Can water
1 ½ Cans rice

Steps:

1. Combine ingredients and put in dish
2. Place chicken pieces on top
3. Bake at 350°F for 60 minutes

Aunt Jean's Seafood Au Gratin

- 3 Tablespoons butter
- 3 Tablespoons flour
- ½ Teaspoon black pepper
- ½ Teaspoon salt
- 1 Cup heavy cream
- 1 Package of seafood (recommend scallops) uncooked
- 1 Teaspoon Worcestershire sauce
- 1 Teaspoon onion juice
- ½ Cup grated Swiss cheese
- ½ Cup buttered cracker crumbs

Steps:

1. Melt butter in sauce pan
2. Add flour
3. Stir over medium heat for 2 minutes; do not let the mixture brown
4. Add cream, salt, pepper, Worcestershire sauce, onion juice
5. Stir till sauce thickens
6. Remove from stove and add uncooked seafood
7. Place in baking dish, top with cheese and crumbs
8. Bake at 350°F for 20 to 25 minutes

Note: Sauce will be very thick but will thin out when baked

Stromboli

1 Loaf frozen bread dough, thawed
1 Pound salami
1 Pound pepperoni
1 Pound provolone cheese
1 Package shredded mozzarella cheese

Steps:

1. Roll out bread dough to fit on cookie sheet (18 x12)
2. Cover dough completely with salami, pepperoni and provolone cheese
4. Alternating and get close to the edge of the dough
5. Sprinkle generously with shredded mozzarella cheese
6. Roll up long side and pinch ends together
7. Pinch and blend sides together
8. Let rise 20 minutes
9. Brush outside with egg and garlic powder
10. Sprinkle outside with sesame
11. Bake at 350^0F for 30 to 40 minutes and do not bake past golden

Chicken Enchiladas

- 4 to 5 Chicken breasts, cooked and chopped
- 3 Tablespoons olive oil
- 1 ½ White onions, chopped
- 5 Cloves garlic
- 1 4 or 6 ounce can diced Ortega green chilies
- ½ Can tomatoes, puree
- 1 Teaspoon chili powder
- 1 Teaspoon cumin
- 1 Package corn tortillas
- 1 Pound Jack cheese
- 1 Pint heavy whipping cream
- 1 Chicken bouillon cube
- Dash of salt and pepper

Steps:

1. Sauté onion and garlic in olive oil until limp
2. Add chicken, chilies, tomato puree and spices
3. Simmer over low heat for about 30 minutes
4. In separate bowl, grate Jack cheese and mix well with whipping cream
5. Crumble chicken bouillon cube and mix well with cheese and cream mixture
6. Heat a small amount of oil in frying pan
7. Cook tortillas quickly on both sides until soft
8. Place 2 to 3 tablespoons of chicken mixture in middle of tortilla and roll
9. Place in Pam-sprayed baking dish
10. After rolling all your enchiladas, pour the cheese mixture over top
11. Bake at 350°F for 35 to 45 minutes, until lightly browned and bubbly

Grandmother's Chicken and Dumplings

- 6 Chicken thighs or 1 whole chicken
- 2 Tablespoons butter
- ¾ Cup, chicken broth
- 1 Package egg noodles (optional)
- 1 Box Bisquick

Steps for cooking chicken:

1. Wash chicken
2. Cook chicken with butter and broth in large covered pot
3. Add about 2 inches of water above chicken
4. Cook for 2 hours or until chicken is tender
5. Remove chicken, cool and debone (can run cold water over chicken to assist in deboning the chicken)
6. Remove about ½ cup broth and set aside
7. After deboning chicken place back in broth and bring to a boil
8. Save a couple pieces of skin to add back into the boiling water
9. In a separate cup, mix flour and water into a paste mixture, until it's a smooth mixture; pour mixture into boiling water with the chicken for a thicker soup

Steps for making dumplings:

1. Add ½ cup broth to eggs
2. Stir in 2 ½ cups of Bisquick mix to make a stiff dough
3. Roll out dough and cut into squares and roll into balls
4. Let dry for 1 hour
5. Drop into boiling broth
6. Cook 10 minutes with lid on and 10 minutes with lid off
7. Cook at medium stove temperature
8. Prepare egg noodles as directed on package
9. Remove dumplings from soup
10. Add the drained egg noodles to soup, stir and put dumplings back in soup
11. Let soup sit for 10 to 15 minutes until soup starts to thicken

Note: Add salt, onions, celery, carrot or other items for additional flavoring

Mother's Pigs in a Blanket

1 Can tomato paste
1 Box white rice
1 Head of cabbage
1 Can of sauerkraut
2 Pounds ground beef
3 Green peppers, chopped

Steps:

1. Fry up ground beef until slightly brown, drain off exceed grease
2. Prepare white rice as directed on box
3. Boil head of cabbage
4. Layer 13 x 9 inch baking dish with tomato paste
5. Remove cabbage leafs
6. Mix rice, ground beef and peppers together
7. On each cabbage leaf, add mixture and roll
8. Pour sauerkraut and extra tomato paste over cabbage leafs
9. Bake at 350^{0}F for 30 to 45 minutes

Miscellaneous Recipes

To keep eggs from popping when you are frying them, sprinkle
a tablespoon of flour or a little cornstarch in the hot
grease and break the eggs into this.
They will also have a better flavor.

Jack's Barbecue Sauce

- 3 Cups water
- 2 Cups vinegar (use 1 cup of water and 1 cup of vinegar, if vinegar is strong)
- ½ Cup sugar
- 2 Small cans tomato paste
- 1 Teaspoon dry mustard
- 1 Teaspoon salt
- 1 Tablespoon chopped onions
- 1 Clove garlic
- ½ Cup Brown sugar

Steps:

1. Mix ingredients together
2. Salt and pepper meat
3. Baste with sauce and refrigerate for 1 to 2 hours, turning meat and rebasting every hour
4. Sauce can be used with either beef or pork
5. Cook for several hours at low heat in oven, basting every 30 minutes, until meat shreds itself

Granddad's Turkey Stuffing

- 3 Tablespoons salad oil
- 2 Large onions, chopped
- 1 Loaf stuffing bread
- 4 Eggs
- 1 Stock of celery tops (about 1 cup)
- Giblets (cut in small pieces)

Steps:

1. Fry onions, giblets and celery tops
2. In the meantime, cut up bread (in small cubes) and soak in milk
3. Then squeeze out and add to the fried mixture
4. Fry until brown
5. Let mixture cool
6. When cool, add eggs and salt and pepper to taste, mixing thoroughly
7. Stuff turkey just before roasting or bake stuffing at 325°F for 45 minutes. Topping with bread crumbs
8. For additional flavoring, add minced-up apples and oranges to this recipe and mix in with the eggs
9. Baste the outside of the turkey with olive oil or butter

Sausage Dressing

- 1 Pound pork sausage
- 9 Cups dry or toasted bread crumbs
- ¼ Teaspoon pepper
- 2 Medium onions, chopped
- 1 ½ Teaspoon salt
- 1 ½ Cups chopped celery

Steps:

1. Combine all ingredients and moisten just slightly with hot water
2. Bake in baking dish at 325°F for 45 to 60 minutes

Ann's Cheese Balls

- 1 5 ounce jar sharp spreading cheese
- ¼ Cup butter or margarine
- ½ Teaspoon salt
- ½ Cup flour

Steps:

1. Cream cheese and butter
2. Add sifted dry ingredients and mix well
3. Form 1 inch balls, place on greased baking sheet
4. Chill about 2 hours or overnight
5. Bake at 400°F for 10 minutes

To Serve:

Great with a fruit salad

Simple Fruit Mixture

- Use cantaloupe or honeydew melon
- Choice of berries, seedless grapes or canned fruit cocktail

Steps:

1. Fill half-inch, pared ring of cantaloupe or honeydew melon with choice of berries, seedless or drained fruit cocktail

To Serve:

1. Fill with ice cream or sherbet

Lena's Italian Salad Dressing

- 5 Cloves garlic
- ½ Onion, chopped
- 1 Teaspoon pepper
- ½ Teaspoon sugar
- 1 Teaspoon lemon
- 1 Can anchovies (oil and all)
- 3 Eggs
- 2 Cups Vesson oil
- 1 Teaspoon mustard

Steps:

1. Using a blender on low and mix in onion, garlic and anchovies
2. Add in sugar, pepper, mustard and lemon
3. Then blend in 1 egg at a time and gradually add oil to the blender mixture

Spinach Balls

3 Packages chopped spinach
6 Eggs
8 Ounces stuffing mixture
⅔ cup melted butter
1 Cup onion, chopped fine
1 Teaspoon garlic powder
1 Teaspoon seasoning salt
1 Teaspoon pepper
1 Cup parmesan cheese

Steps:

1. Cook spinach as per package directions
2. Drain well, getting most of the water out
3. Lightly mix eggs, butter and stuffing, softening and breaking down bread (recommend crush the stuffing cubes prior to mixing)
4. Thoroughly stir in all other ingredients
5. Make into 1 inch balls
6. Bake on cookie sheet at 350°F for 20 to 30 minutes
7. Can make in advance and freeze first then bake later

Pastries and Pies

Smell the aroma of pies baking in the oven. Bring your ice cream and fork to the table and enjoy these delightful pastries and pies from grandmothers' kitchen.

Aunt Joan's Pumpkin Chiffon Pie

- 6 Eggs
- 1 ½ Cups cooked pumpkin
- ½ Teaspoon salt
- ½ Teaspoon nutmeg
- ¼ Cup cold water
- ½ Cup granulated sugar
- ¾ Cup brown sugar
- ½ Cup milk
- 1 Teaspoon cinnamon
- 1 Envelope Knox gelatin

Steps:

1. Combine 3 beaten egg yolks, brown sugar, pumpkin, milk, salt and spices
2. Cook in double boiler until thick, stirring constantly
3. Soak gelatin in cold water, stir into hot mixture
4. Chill until partly set
5. Then beat in separate bowl 3 egg whites, adding granulated sugar and beat stiff
6. Fold this mixture into gelatin mixture
7. Pour into pie shell and chill until set

To Serve:

1. Garnish with whipped cream

Yield: Makes 1 large pie or 8 individual pies

Pineapple Cheese Pie

- 1 6 ounce can (⅔ Cup) evaporated milk
- 1 Cup crushed pineapple
- ¼ Cup sugar
- ½ Teaspoon salt
- 1 Egg
- 1 Package lemon flavored gelatin
- 1 Cup large curd cream cottage cheese
- 1 9 inch graham cracker crust

Steps:

1. Chill milk, beater and bowl
2. Combine the pineapple, sugar, salt and egg in saucepan; cook over low heat till thickened, stirring constantly
3. Remove from heat and add gelatin; stir till dissolved; chill till partially set or mounds when spooned
4. Beat evaporated milk till light and fluffy
5. Fold in gelatin mixture and cottage cheese
6. Pile into graham cracker crust and chill until firm

To Serve:

1. Garnish with pineapple slices and maraschino cherries just before serving

Strawberry Cream Pie

- 1 Quart strawberries (sugar and let stand until juicy)
- 1 3 ounce package cream cheese
- ½ Cup powdered sugar
- ½ Teaspoon vanilla
- ½ Teaspoon almond extract
- ½ Pint whipped cream
- 1 Tablespoon cornstarch
- Few drops of red food coloring

Steps:

1. Cream the cheese and add the sugar and flavoring
2. Fold into this mixture whipping cream
3. Add this mixture into a cooled and pre-baked 9 inch pie shell baked
4. Let this chill for about 30 minutes
5. Glaze 1 cup of liquid (juice plus water to equal this amount)
6. Add cornstarch and a few drops of red food coloring
7. Cook until thick and clear
8. Then add strawberries and cool separately
9. Pour on top of cream that is chilled and return to refrigerator

Brownie Pie

- 3 Egg whites
- ¾ Cup sugar
- ¾ Cup fine chocolate wafer crumbs
- ½ Cup chopped walnuts (optional)
- Dash of salt

Steps:

1. Beat egg whites and salt, gradually adding sugar until stiff
2. Mix with chocolate crumbs and walnuts (optional)
3. Spread evenly in lightly butter 9 inch pie dish
4. Bake at 325°F for 35 minutes
5. Cool thoroughly
6. Spread with sweetened whipped cream
7. Chill well, 3 to 4 hours

To Serve:

1. Trim with curls of shaved chocolate

Chocolate Pie

- 4 Milk chocolate candy bars
- 16 Medium marshmallows
- ½ Cup milk
- ½ Pint cream

Steps:

1. Melt chocolate and marshmallows in milk
2. Add cream
3. Freeze in prebaked pie shell for several hours

John's Custard Pie

- 3 Eggs, slightly beaten
- ½ Cup granulated sugar
- 2 ⅓ Cups hot milk
- ½ Teaspoon vanilla

Steps:

1. Mix in all ingredients
2. Beat with rotary beater until foamy
3. Pour in unbaked pastry shell
4. Sprinkle lightly with nutmeg
5. Bake at 425°F for 20 minutes and then reduce heat to 325°F for 20 minutes

Ann's Banana Wheat Germ Muffins

- ⅓ Cup shortening
- ⅔ Cup sugar
- 2 Eggs
- 1 ½ Cups flour
- 2 Teaspoons baking powder
- ¼ Teaspoon baking soda
- ¼ Cup sour milk
- ½ Teaspoon salt
- 1 Cup wheat germ
- ¾ Cup mashed bananas

Steps:

1. Cream shortening, add sugar and eggs
2. Beat flour and dry ingredients except wheat germ
3. Then add wheat germ
4. Combine bananas and sour milk
5. Stir in alternately liquid with dry ingredients
6. Fill muffin tins ⅔ full
7. Bake at 400°F for 25 minutes

Yields: 1 dozen

Blueberry Cobbler

- 2 Cups blueberries
- 4 Tablespoons sugar
- 1 Cup flour
- 1 Teaspoon baking powder
- ½ Teaspoon salt
- ½ Cup sugar
- 1 Egg, beaten
- ¼ Cup milk
- ½ Teaspoon vanilla
- 2 Teaspoons butter

Steps:

1. Place blueberries in cover dish (1 quart casserole, well greased)
2. Sprinkle berries with 4 tablespoons sugar
3. Sift dry ingredient
4. Combine egg, milk, vanilla and melted butter
5. Stir enough to combine
6. Spread mixture over blueberries
7. Bake at 350^0F for 30 minutes

Salads

If eggs to be boiled are cracked, add a little vinegar or a teaspoon of salt to the water and the egg whites will not come out. Boiling eggs in salt water also makes them peel more easily if they are placed in cold water after boiling.

Molded Potato Salad

- 1 ½ Cups water
- 2 Tablespoons instant minced onions
- 1 Envelope instant mashed potato
- ¼ Cup mustard
- ¼ Cup mayonnaise
- 1 Cup diced celery
- ¼ Cup diced green peppers
- 2 Tablespoons chopped sweet pickle
- 1 Tablespoon pimento
- 2 Chopped hard boiled eggs
- ½ Teaspoon salt

Steps:

1. Bring water to boil
2. Remove, add minced onion and stir in instant mashed potato
3. Mix in mustard and mayonnaise and blend into hot potatoes
4. Then add in remaining ingredients
5. Brush 1 ½ quart mold with salad oil, line with strips of green pepper, 2 sliced hard boiled eggs and sliced olives
6. Gently press salad into mold and chill

Serves 8

Refrigerator Salad

1 Can diced pineapple pieces
1 Can mandarin oranges
1 Box coconut
1 Package small marshmallows
1 Pint sour cream

Steps:

1. Mix the above ingredients and place in baking dish
2. Refrigerate for 12 hours and serve

Cinnamon Candy Salad

1 Package cherry Jello
1 Cup hot water
¼ Cup red cinnamon candies
½ Cup boiling water
1 Cup chopped apples
1 Cup chopped celery
½ Cup chopped walnuts (optional)

Steps:

1. Dissolve Jello in cup of hot water
2. Add candies to ½ cup boiling water, stir till dissolved
3. Add water to make 1 cup
4. Then add mixture to Jello
5. Cool until partially set and add other ingredients
6. Chill and serve

Cranberry Chiffon Salad

- 1 Small package Philadelphia cream cheese
- 1 Package lemon Jello
- 1 Cup boiling water
- 1 Can cooked cranberry sauce, whole berries
- ½ Pint whipping cream

Steps:

1. Dissolve the Jello in boiling water and allow it to cool
2. When it begins to jell whip until fluffy with rotary beater
3. Break down cheese with fork and add with whipped cream
4. Then add cranberries and stir altogether
5. Chill for several hours

Serves 8

Coca-Cola Salad

- 1 8 ounce package cream cheese (cut in small chunks)
- 1 Can dark sweet cherries, drained
- 1 Can pineapple chunks, drained
- 2 Bottles Coca-Cola
- 2 Packages of cherry Jello

Steps:

1. Heat the juice from the cherries and pineapple
2. Dissolve Jello in heated juice and add Coca-Colas and let chill slightly
3. Then add cherries, pineapple and cream cheese and chill until set
4. Use 13 x 9 inch baking dish

To Serve:

1. Serve on lettuce with salad dressing as a salad or with whipped cream as a dessert

Pineapple Salad

- 1 Cup crushed pineapple, drained
- 1 Cup sugar
- 1 Envelope plain gelatin
- 1 Cup American cheese, grated
- 1 Cup miracle whip
- ½ Pint whipping cream, whipped
- 1 Lemon, juice

Steps:

1. Mix crushed pineapple, sugar and lemon juice boiling for 3 minutes
2. Add plain gelatin that has been dissolved in ½ cup cold water
3. Cool until jelled
4. Then beat until frothy and add grated cheese, miracle whip and whipping cream
5. Fold together well
6. Place in 13 x 9 inch baking dish
7. Chill for several hours

Sandwiches

If in a hurry, here are a few quick and easy sandwiches
to feed the hungry kids and family.

Stuffed Pups

- 1 Package hot dogs
- 1 Package cream cheese
- 2 Tomatoes
- ½ Pound Bacon

Steps:

1. Split each hot dog lengthwise and place a strip of cream cheese in the opening
2. Wrap with slice of bacon and secure with meat skewers or toothpicks
3. Arrange on broiler pan with tomato slices (seasoned with a little butter)
4. Place broiler pan so that meat is 3 inches from unit
5. Broil 6 to 8 minutes, turning several times
6. Serve on hot dog buns

Creole Burgers

- 1 Pound ground beef
- 1 Can chicken gumbo soup
- 1 Small onion, chopped
- 2 Tablespoons mustard
- 2 Tablespoons ketchup
- ¼ Teaspoon pepper

Steps:

1. Brown beef and onion
2. Add remaining ingredients and mix well
3. Cook until onion is tender
4. Serve on hamburger buns

Yields: Approximately 8 to 10 burgers

Bean Burger

- 6 Round buns
- 2 Tablespoon ketchup
- 1 Can condensed bean with bacon soup
- 1 Tablespoon minced onion
- 4 Hot dogs

Steps:

1. Split the buns in half
2. Combine ketchup, soup, and onions
3. Spread rather thickly on the cut side of buns
4. Slice hot dogs into round ¼ inch thick pieces
5. Arrange hot dogs slices on the buns
6. Broil 8 to 10 minutes

Yields: 12 burgers

Deviled Egg Burgers

- 1 Package round buns
- 1 Can deviled ham
- 6 Scrambled eggs
- 1 Package Velveeta cheese

Steps:

1. Cut round buns in half; toast cut side
2. Spread each bun half with deviled ham
3. Top first with scrambled eggs then with grated Velveeta cheese
4. Place in oven until warm through
5. For finishing touch, place under broiler to melt cheese

Onionburgers

- 1 Pound ground beef
- 2 Tablespoon flour
- 1 Can onion soup

Steps:

1. Brown ground beef in a heavy skillet, stirring to separate meat particles
2. Sprinkle flour over meat; stir until well mixed with the meat
3. Add onion soup; cook until thoroughly heated and slightly thickened

Yields: 8 burgers

Soups

Here are the delightful soup recipes for those winter meals.

Bean Soup

- ½ Package white beans
- 1 Ham bone
- 1 ½ Cups diced potatoes
- 2 Cups diced celery
- 1 Large diced onion
- 1 Can tomato sauce
- 1 small can of tomatoes

Steps:

1. Soak ham bone and white beans in water all night
2. Start in a.m. and cook slowly for 3 or 4 hours
3. Remove bone
4. Add diced potatoes, diced celery, diced onion, tomato sauce and tomatoes
5. Add seasoning for taste
6. Cook on low heat for 30 minutes

New England Corn Crowder

- 1 Cup diced potatoes
- 2 Tablespoons chopped onion
- 2 Strips bacon
- 1 Pint milk
- 1 Can cream style corn

Steps:

1. Cook bacon until light brown, add onion
2. Cook 3 minutes, stirring, add in potatoes and milk
3. Add dash of salt and pepper for taste
4. Bring to boil and cook gently, uncovered for 20 minutes
5. Stir in corn
6. Bring to boil and serve

Egg Drop Soup

- 1 Cup beef bouillon
- 1 Soup can of water or 2 cups chicken broth
- 1 Egg, slightly beaten
- $\frac{1}{8}$ Teaspoon salt

Steps:

1. Heat soup and water to boiling
2. Combine egg and salt
3. Pour mixture through a fine strainer into the boiling soup, moving strainer back and forth so egg falls into soup in fine threads
4. Cook 1 minute

Yields: 2 ½ cups of soup

John's Barley Soup

- ½ Cup barley
- 1 Teaspoon salt
- 1 Quart boiling water
- 2 Quarts soup stock
- ½ Cup diced celery
- ½ Cup diced onions
- ½ Cup diced carrots
- 1 Green pepper, diced

Steps:

1. Wash barley in cold water and cook in boiling salt water until tender, about 2 hours
2. Adding soup stock when water has evaporated
3. Add vegetables half hour before soup is done

Yields: Serving for 6

Fall Soup

- 1 Pound ground beef
- 1 Cup onion, chopped
- 4 Cups water
- 1 Cup cut-up carrots
- 1 Cut cut-up potatoes
- 1 Teaspoon Kitchen Bouquet Sauce
- 1 28 ounce can tomatoes with liquid
- 2 Teaspoon salt
- 1 Bay leaf
- ¼ Teaspoon pepper or oregano
- 1 Cup chopped celery

Steps:

1. Use a large sauce pan, cook and stir beef until brown
2. Drain off fat
3. Add onions and cook until tender, about 5 minutes
4. Add all other ingredients
5. Bring to a boil
6. Reduce heat and cover and simmer about 60 minutes

Yields: Serving for 6

Made in the USA
San Bernardino, CA
04 November 2012